REMEMBER THIS DAY

poems by

Linda Drattell

Finishing Line Press
Georgetown, Kentucky

REMEMBER THIS DAY

ACKNOWLEDGMENTS

Warm thanks to the following publications in which these poems or an
earlier version of them first appeared:

Prompt for the Planet, Viewless Wings Publisher: "The Torrent and the Tree"
Viewless Wings Publisher: "Old Man;" "Paddington Park"
Wingless Dreamer, Field of Black Roses anthology: "When Your Heart No
Longer Beats"
Las Positas College, *Havik* anthology: "Compassion;" "The Who That You
Are"

I want to thank my husband, Eric, for his endless support and willingness
to read my writings *just one more time*, despite the fact he insists poetry
is not his thing. A big thank-you to my children, Michael and Alexandra,
and to my daughter-in-law, Angel, for being much-needed sounding
boards. Gratitude to Constance Handstedt, James Morehead, Patricia Boyle,
Monique Rardin Richardson, Marie-Anne Poudret, Marilyn Dykstra,
Eun Hee Soh, Ida Marie Beck, Matthew Felíx, Bruce Wawrzyniak, and
the California Writers Club Tri-Valley Chapter for their support and
encouragement.

Publisher: Leah Huete de Maines
Editor: Christen Kincaid
Cover Art: Monique Rardin Richardson
Author Photo: Monique Rardin Richardson
Interior Art: Shawn Drattell
Cover Design: Elizabeth Maines McCleavy

Order online: www.finishinglinepress.com
                also available on amazon.com

Author inquiries and mail orders:
Finishing Line Press
PO Box 1626
Georgetown, Kentucky 40324
USA

Table of Contents

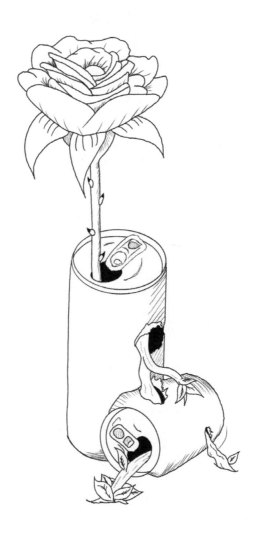

For my husband, Eric

The Torrent and the Tree

Why does it struggle so?
Its branches tremble and shiver
against that which will inevitably
overcome it.

The biting rain flogs its leaves,
the raw wind mauls its branches.
The irate river, pulsing and rupturing the embankment,
whips up slumbering silt and loosens the hold of its roots.
Lawless rapids sweep around it triumphantly,
dragging the tree to a slow prostrate death.

Yet it resists, as if sheer will
can repel the forces which assault it.
A few extra minutes of life, worth the agony.
The tree twists and twines with a pluck it did not know it possessed,
its impaled soul refuses the sweet death that beckons.

It seems to know why it is there.
Its defiant arms are streaked with rugged lines
from splintering cracks,
its trunk scarred with raw nubs
where young branches fanning budding leaves
once grasped the sky.

As it sinks to the will of the aggressor,
the trembling forest bears witness,
comprehends it is the tree
which has overcome the torrential waters.

Its measure,
Now resting in long-overdue quietude,
gazes gratefully at Heaven
for not even Death can erase
those precious defiant moments it spent on Earth.

When Your Heart No Longer Beats

I know one day you will take your last breath
Leave me and grasp the cold hand of death
I want you to touch me as you pass on
Leave your fingers' impress after you've gone

Pillows behind you
Quilt on your lap
I'll stroke your head gently
Pretend it's a nap

Your head will nod slowly as if you agree
I cannot survive this—it should have been me
To go first.
I should have been first.

Old Man

White hairs pepper his sepia forehead below a thinned black mane.
They cover the nether side of his throat like an old man's goatee,
light eyeshadow near dark eyes still large and curious,
a chalky accent along the lean muscle of his neck,
a patch here and there above his fetlocks, the side of one hock.
War injuries, not age, the erectness of his posture suggests.

The winter months are approaching,
a time of year when he quickly loses heft.
I monitor his eating closely, watch him slowly nibble his grain,
prod him to eat more.
His muzzle works methodically,
slipping food past worn molars no longer capable of chewing.

The farrier laughs when she comes to trim his hooves.
Nothing to trim, she says,
He shuffles like an old man.
His hind legs cross as he rambles.
I watch him head slowly to the far corner of the field
then double back at a happy gait,
not exactly a run,
proud of his stride, nonetheless.

He has a thing for the mares,
neighs, expects them to respond—
they glance at him for a second, go back to grazing.
He makes an effort to rear up,
tries to jump the fence separating him from them
though he'd been gelded ages ago.
Perhaps he's forgotten.
He has an agenda.
Dirty old man, the barn manager calls him.

I remember how we used to ride through lush east coast forest,
sail through the air over fallen logs,
pass between trees with barely enough space for his torso and my legs,
eat mulberries from low-hanging branches,
avoid stinging nettle.
Once, we encountered a lone hiker with a monstrous backpack the color
of algae—

a fast lope brought to an abrupt stop,
a surprised hello,
her warning about a copperhead poking his head out of the creek.

I look at his frail legs and am reminded of the year he foundered,
coffin bone twisted in the hoof,
padded high-heeled horseshoes,
special diet,
minimal exercise.

I remember the lightning complex fires,
his evacuation,
the helicopters,
the pregnant cow escaping the stall next to his.

I don't know how much longer I'll have him.
Arthritis is rearing its own ugly head.
Still, he shows off a feisty side usually kept well-hidden.
Some have suggested I need to let him go,
the winter will be very hard,
loss is a part of life.

He looks up from his bucket of grain,
gazes at me with kind eyes.
A bit rusty but I've still got it in me, he says,
give me a second.
He presses his muzzle against my cheek, a kiss.
Old age is nothing, he reassures me.

Compassion

In
a grassy field
shared with an aging bay horse
four goats, two Nigerian and two Nubian
of different mothers, form an unlikely herd. The undeveloped
stretch where they run and forage rolls boundless, pristine pasture
purchased by a man who thought he would build on it,
but the land lies in a flood plain, so
the field remains as virginal
as the day he
bought
it.

The
four goats who
claim this field want their necks
stroked, ears scratched, that soft spot at the base
of the V between their racks rubbed, but don't mistake
them for docile creatures. They will fight fiercely for snacks offered,
clash brutally, bash foreheads, lock curved white horns, attack with whiter teeth
for a banana peel or piece of carrot or Fig Newton cookie.
They battle over the scant shade offered beneath
sparse boughs and the narrow awning
shielding the old
horse's feed
bin.

Nutmeg,
the black and beige goat
with angular horns jutting like two boomerangs,
holds sway over the other three goats. Lately, he suffers
debilitating arthritis in his legs, his joints have lost their agency,
his bones struggle to work in tandem, the links between them broken.
His right front leg resists any attempt to put weight on it,
causing him to trip and fall, even at a slow pace,
move forward with
an abnormal
hop.

He
has become thin,
can barely forage despite the
lush green of the plain and the autumnal leaves
tumbling from the oak tree in the middle of the field.
He is attacked by two of the others. The fourth goat, having
no hope of competing, minds his place, observes
quietly as one of the contenders
hammers his horns into
Nutmeg's
side.

Yet,
as the night
falls to freezing temperatures,
the other goats follow Nutmeg to where
he chooses to rest, nestle around him oblivious
to horse and goat manure, use the
warmth of their bodies
to shield him from
the icy
wind.

pigweed

proud displays of circular
verdant leaves on skinny stems which
horses won't eat but are a delicacy for the
cows have taken over the grassy pasture invaded it
with a vengeance leaving little room for grass to grow
black angus cows are eating the pigweed they have been
brought in for only that purpose to enjoy the smorgasbord
of round leaves on thin shoots while the horses wait to eat
the grass hidden beneath presently out of reach—a child's
swing hangs from the branch of an ancient oak tree in
the middle of the field the oak must be hundreds of
years old judging by the size of its trunk and
the stretch of its gnarly branches one fat
cow has gone over to the swing he's
rubbing his head against
it lets it
roll
off
his
back
I
want
to
yell
focus
eat
the
pigweed
Eat
eat
eat
all
of
it.

Nutmeg's Jacket

I feed my goat extra grain
in an effort to help him
keep on weight
which he loses anyway
like loose change through
a hole in one's pocket.
The farm manager is worried
about the freezing temperatures
and has made him a jacket.

This jacket is impressive
thick plaid cloth
with leather piping
lined for warmth.
It covers his shoulders
reaches midway down his sides.
Stitching shows where to center it
along his back.
A mozzetta of sorts.

The grain
is not fattening him.
The jacket
secured by Velcro closures
keeps coming undone
and constantly falls
to the wayside
like so many good intentions.

Tempest

Rain slashes parallel to the bespattered sodden field
piercing darts propelled by unruly wind.
The ground, a spongy bald expanse
where grass once grew but died in the drought,
allows a horse's weight to leave watery hoofprints
sufficiently deep for frogs to lay their eggs,
if there were any, there aren't any.
The rain has come too late,
too much at once.
The media calls it a "bomb cyclone,"
an "atmospheric river event."
Over the course of one day
an empty barrel in my backyard
collects six inches of rainwater.

I drive to the farm past fallen tree branches,
steer carefully through gale winds,
grab my horse's soaked nylon halter
from the top rung of the pasture's steel enclosure,
run through the downpour to the middle of the field
where Vegas stands quietly
and place the halter over his graying face.
I lead him,
thinned aging shadow of him,
to the warmth of the barn
and offer him grain in one of the dry stalls.

He balks,
grunts a vexed snort,
thrashes his neck,
kicks the side of the barn with his left front hoof,
disgusted with limits set by others.
He refuses the grain,
refuses my touch,
rears up at the horse in the stall next to his.

He wants nothing to do with the barn,
prefers the freedom of the pasture
in the maelstrom.
He calms down when I lead him back outside
into the stinging rain,
the wind whipping around us.

Paddington Park

We lived for a time in London's Marylebone neighborhood
On Chiltern Street, a stone's throw from Paddington Park
It rains most of the time in London regardless
of the time of year—my husband says this
is what he loves most about London
you appreciate when the sun
does come out

Our dog loved our walks
through Paddington Park, probably
because of the other dogs he would meet
A variety of roses grow robustly there, probably
because of the incessant rain and the city's tending
Benches are dedicated to people who have passed away
who once declared this to be their beloved park, probably
because they took refuge there from rushing to work, rushing home

On one of our strolls through the park I noticed a heavyset man
slumped on one of the benches, his eyes closed
his body rumpled beneath a pressed shirt
I thought he was sleeping, perhaps he
had grown tired from walking
Then I realized
he had died

Two police officers
arriving at the same conclusion
tried to waken him—one left to seek help
the other sat next to the man as if they were friends
solidarity through gentle touching, shoulder to shoulder
a macabre camaraderie, the deceased unaware of the living presence
How lonely the man must have been when he chose to sit on that bench

I looked away and continued past the rose bushes and other benches
past a children's play area, exited the park, strolled along
Marylebone High Street and stopped by a café
drank a cup of hot tea at an outside table
my dog patiently curled by my feet
thought of the man on the bench
How lonely death is
no matter the
setting

Almost
an hour later
I circled back through the park
and noticed the same police officer
still seated by the dead man, eyeing the park entrance
for his partner to return. We both nodded, sucked our lips
into a half pout, as if we worked for the same miserable boss, no
idea when help would arrive. How lonely death is, no matter the weather

Stride

I am sprinting through the park
Not the pace I used to run
but it feels good
The breeze brushing against my skin
warms in the sunlight
turns cool in the shade of oak trees
The sidewalk feels solid beneath my feet

I can't compete
with that squirrel's jeté in the air
its back arched
its feet poised
its weight shifted effortlessly to its forelegs
as it leaps across the grass with an acorn to bury

Nor is my step as quick
as that little one's glide
cruising past on his starter bike
steering small donut wheels
looking as if he only recently learned to walk
small legs in starter shorts and starter sneakers

I cannot keep up
With the stride of that man walking by
without a hint of gray in his black hair
long legs in comfortable jeans
taut cheekbones and a tense jaw
not yet etched by life
listening to something he disagrees with
through his earbuds

I lag behind
the boy on his skateboard
hair catching the wind
tee shirt puffed
sneakers maintaining traction
his arms now raised like a seagull in flight
a jump of skateboard and skater
in defiance of gravity
landing again without missing a beat

Even so
I zip past a couple
wearing wide-brimmed hats
holding hands
more interested in each other
than moving forward

My pace is mine
endorphin heaven

Focus

A brother and sister laugh
run through the park
delight in the feel of the grass
between their toes
skip in the shade of evergreen trees
pick up pinecones
egg each other on
not even school age
yet ready to conquer the world.
Each holds a twig raised like a flag
waves it through the warm spring breeze
their faces shining
as they skip joyfully to their mother
who focuses on her cell phone.

The children raise their arms
to embrace her
then bend them slightly
at the elbow
a weakened reach.
Realizing she doesn't see them
they change course
shift away from her
slow their gaits
call to her half-heartedly
as they pass.

Pace

I am running through the park along
the sidewalk that encircles a wide-open field
where young boys chase a soccer ball
and young dogs chase each other.
They say the first thing to go is taste and smell
followed by loss of breath.
I inhale the thick fragrance of freshly cut grass
delighted I can still detect it
savor it
be infused by it.

A group of women ambles toward me
crowds the sidewalk with conversation.
One of them sees me
weighs whether
to fill the remaining breadth of concrete
to stay in step with her friends
or allow me to pass.
She chooses to reject sidewalk etiquette
skips forward
affirms her right to flock
after months of isolation.
Unhappy at the inconvenience
my right foot lands on grass.
I wait as the group proceeds past me
in murmuration
step back onto the sidewalk
regain my pace.

Turf War

Epi glottis
                      A friend of mine
        From the glottis family
Passed away
Recently
                  While fighting with
        His dear friend,   eso phagus
          From the phagus family
Over a morsel of bread
Till
        He
Choked
        Up
And
Died.

The Who That You Are

You know who you are
When you surrender pretense
When you stop self-assessing
Stuck on past tense
When you realize your life
Isn't all that intense

As you think it must be.

You relinquish all defense
Because none is needed
Agency's your voucher
Best simply to heed it.
When you shed the frayed mask
Then you'll have succeeded

In setting yourself free.

The Tennis Ball

Smashed
          Unscrupulously, contemptuously,
                    Across the net,

                                                            BOUNCE!

BOUNCE!
To
          Win the
                    Serve,
                              The Game,
                                                  The
                                        Set.

                                                            BOUNCE!

BOUNCE!
Misused, brow-beaten,
          Obliged
                    With remiss,

                                                            BOUNCE!

BOUNCE!
          Its function
                    In life
                              To
Be hit
          Or
                    Be missed.

                                                            BOUNCE!
                                                            BOUNCE
                                                            Bounce
                                                            Bounce.

Promenade des Anglais

The man settled in the chair opposite us is unconvincingly cheerful,
affecting a smile as he asks about our travels.
Ah, Paris, the galleries! The Louvre! The Seine!
Diplomas in psychology decorating the wall above his desk,
designed to give him credence as judge and jury of our trauma,
cast doubt within me, an unhealthy skepticism
that he has adequate answers.

His thinning hair, the color of wheat, grasps parched skin.
A rounded stomach from apparent lack of exercise,
perhaps due to too much time in the chair,
the etched furrows between saddened eyes,
and a set jaw despite his attempts to release its grin,
all suggest he has treated too much trauma
over the course of his career.
Yet we came to him for strength we don't have ourselves.

Our sessions with him are as blurred in my mind
as a chalk drawing on the sidewalk after a rainfall.
I lost my hearing decades ago, so
my ability to follow his repartee is difficult,
perhaps that's the reason.

How was Aix en Provence,
Parc National des Calanques, so lovely?
We were vigilant, we say, recalling the Bataclan theater.
And France's win in the semi-final Euro futbol game,
wasn't that something?
Yes, we agree.
We attended the Paris Pride celebration, we add,
expressed our support as allies given the attack
three weeks earlier at an Orlando nightclub.

And Nice!
Yes, we give in, every day warm and sunny,
lunches on the beach,
strolls along the Promenade des Anglais,
the Euro finals between France and Portugal.
The man and Eric chat about their favorite teams,
which players they follow.

Futbol? We're talking about futbol?
My husband's forced laugh shakes me,
I want to shake them both.

Finally, finally,
the man allows us to reveal our purpose.
The day before Bastille Day, my husband recounts,
he suffered a kidney stone but refused an operation,
a decision he believes saved my life.
Because then we had dinner together on the beach
in a lovely restaurant below the Promenade,
watched the Bastille Day fireworks
over white wine and salads and rolls and grilled salmon.

Alone, I would have watched the performance of
lighted fountains against the black sky
with the buoyant crowd above,
stood near the pop-up bandstand
to feel the beat of the music,
bought candy from a nearby street vendor.
I would not have eaten dinner in a restaurant by myself.

And so there we were, sitting at a table
sheathed with a spotless white tablecloth,
solid wooden flooring shielding our feet
from the stony pebbled shore,
an olive-green awning buffering us
from the cacophony above, tranquil.

We finished our dinner, we explain,
ready to join the festive crowd on the street,
waited for our bill.
Our server accepted payment first
from a heavyset gentleman and his wife—
fellow guests from our hotel—
untanned, new arrivals perhaps,
each dressed in casual shirts and shorts,
vacationers like us.
We watched them climb the wooden steps
to the Promenade des Anglais,
anxious to leave ourselves.

My husband glanced toward the awning;
something caught his eye.
I followed his gaze.
People were diving headfirst
off the Promenade
onto the restaurant's canopy.
How silly, he remarked.

I couldn't tell when the band music stopped,
didn't hear the rush of the truck
or the screams.
I did hear popping sounds—
seems they were of a frequency
I could still detect—
grabbed my husband's wrist, shouted,
Gunshots!

I pulled him toward bathrooms
hidden by the kitchen.
Someone fell on top of me,
tore my hand from my husband's,
injured my shoulder.
Found my balance,
ran forward without him,
without thinking,
stopped,
looked back,
watched the slow motion of
him walking oddly
from the effects of the
kidney stone
and narcotic pain killers,
a growing crowd
catching up from behind.
I fluttered my hand,
Hurry!
I lipread,
I'm coming, I'm coming.

In a narrow bathroom stall
we joined eight others.
A horde of people pounded
against the steel door
we closed behind us,
trying to get in.
No more room.
Two young girls
crouched on the floor,
knobby knees,
one with her hands pressed
over her ears.
Another girl sat
on the lid of the commode,
legs tucked under her.
A husband and wife,
their doe-eyed son,
two teenage girls separated
from their family,
my husband and me.

One of the teenagers began to cry.
I placed my hand on her shoulder, but
she didn't flinch from my touch,
might not have felt my hand at all.

I kick myself.
Such a debilitating sense of guilt.
I had decided where we should run,
a dead end,
nowhere else to flee
if attackers followed.
Nothing you could have done differently,
no better choice you could have made,
says the man in the chair.
In the heat of the moment
nothing felt like a choice,
yet at the same time
I felt I had free will
and that the decision where to run
had been mine.

From the bathroom stall I texted
our son and daughter,
while my husband posted on Twitter.
News correspondents
picked up his tweets,
asked to interview him.
Why? I'm hiding in a bathroom.
You are coherent and in place.

Our son wrote back,
asked questions.
Our daughter, performing
on a cruise ship,
had not seen the texts.
Someone alerted her.
She heard *your dad* and *terror attack*
in the same sentence,
ran to a television,
checked her phone,
saw 27 missed messages.

I texted my brother,
realized it was a workday.
You must be working.
Not anymore.

We learned a truck
packed with explosives
had run down cheerful strollers,
stopped almost directly above us,
the driver defined more by mental illness
and a history of violent behavior
than by religious affiliation.

I smelled a foul odor that evening
I never experienced before or since,
a mustiness inhaled,
a putridness on my tongue,
rotted dreams.
I sent my children what I thought

was a video of myself
expressing my infinite love for them.
Just in case.
But I'd forgotten suddenly
how to make a video,
inadvertently sent a still photo
of me not looking my best.

We emerged when it was deemed safe,
walked along the pebbly beach
back up to the Promenade.

Bodies sheathed in white tablecloths
taken from nearby restaurants, including ours,
littered the road as far as the eye could see,
like a Stephen King horror flick.
One man could not find his wife,
searched for her under each of those cruel covers,
found her later, alive, but
now would live with what he'd seen.

86 people killed,
including ten children,
Over 400 injured,
including the husband and wife from our hotel,
a crushed baby stroller,
the baby crumpled beside it,
a bicycle,
the body of the teenager who had ridden it.
Police officers shaking
as they frisked us,
went through our bags,
pointed their guns ready to shoot.

Move, hon.
I pressed my husband's arm.
What?
You're standing...
Oh God.
Someone's blood.

Our hotel room overlooked the Promenade.
No escape, no desire to sleep.

In the morning news media continued
their pursuit of my husband,
hounds after a wounded fox.

Explain what happened.
What went through your mind?
Look at the camera.
Speak into the mic.
The retelling over and over,
too much.
One reporter had covered a
suicide bombing in Afghanistan.
No amount of preparation
could have stopped the attacker,
he confided,
Despite what people think.

We flew to London,
called the restaurant.
We haven't paid our bill yet.

My husband says he forever
wants me in his foxhole,
believes I led him to safety.
I led us to a place with no escape,
I say.
You can't look back and think,
I could have, should have…
says the man in the chair.

Sometimes at night I see Death
marching near the foot of my bed,
a robotic Mr. Bean,
arms and knees bent,
jerking closer with each mechanical step,
the lifeless whites of unseeing eyes
as bright as the white socks poking out
from beneath a black business suit
not quite reaching the ankles.

In photographs my husband took of me
before that evening
I'm smiling,
my brown hair mussed by the wind,
a drink in my hand,
gazing flirtatiously.
It's hard for me
to look at these photographs,
myself as yet unaware.

We survived, but why?
Were we privileged because we were lucky,
or were we lucky because we were privileged?
Dinner at a lovely beach restaurant
Waiting to pay our bill.

There is a Buddhist parable
that speaks of being shot
by two arrows
when we suffer from tragedy.
The second arrow,
our reaction to the first arrow,
is more painful.
The second arrow is optional.
This is what the man in the chair
wants us to understand,
why he asks no questions
about the attack,
why he wants us
to think of other things.

Trauma creates a gravel road in our brains.
Thinking too much about what happened
widens that gravel road
into an asphalt street,
and that asphalt street
into an eight-lane highway.

I avoid crowds these days.
Always keep my phone charged.
Every so often, my husband and I cry.

July 14, 2016.
I am slowly forgetting the date.
Then a similar attack occurs elsewhere,
another date.
How do we know when we are healed—
when we no longer fall apart at the news?

Hunt

The wolves are hungry.
They've been tracking
for a while now
over thick snow.
Wide four-toed paws
snowshoeing in tandem
across the belly of the valley.
Leaden skies have dusted
their thick gray and black fur
with white flocculent jackets
as pale as the markings
on their faces and underbellies,
thick crusts of snow on their backs
that don't melt under the scarce
sunlight cutting in and out
from behind shifting shutters
like a battery on the brink of dying.

They are hungry.
They are hunting.
They've covered a large territory.
They find the bison.

The bison are foraging.
They swish their immense heads
back and forth to disperse the snow,
scouring for grasses, leaves, twigs, bark,
anything edible.
They notice the wolves.
Burly dark brown coats
are drawn taut.
They grunt,
stand firm side by side,
one massive collective beast
brandishing sharp horns
and deadly hooves,
impenetrable.

The wolves encircle the herd,
wait patiently.
This standoff could last days.

Eventually, the bison separate,
charge to defend.
The wolves separate,
search for a weakness.
One of the wolves
catches a young bison,
matches his speed,
grabs hold with powerful jaws,
tears into the tender flesh
of the immature flank,
releases it to avoid the calf's kicks,
grabs hold again,
again,
again,
and again.

The wolf relies
on other members of the pack
to keep the rest of the herd at bay.
The young bison slows.
The wolf's jaws hold firm
until the calf, ungracefully,
falls in the snow.

A large bull turns,
lowers its behemothic head,
thrusts the full measure of its bulk,
uses the strength and agility
it has gained
from years of practice
surviving and adapting
to the predator-prey relationship,
charges the wolf
with the sharp curve of its horns,
convinces the predator
to seek easier prey.

The wolf releases the calf.
The kill, for now,
is thwarted.

The wolves must try again,
must eat,
must find another bison
to sustain kith and kin,
driven solely by hunger,
their need to survive,
nothing more.

Linda Drattell is a poet and writer from Northern California. She has lived and worked in three world capitals on three continents and draws from her lifetime of experiences to inform her writing. She earned a bachelor's degree in social work from the Hebrew University in Jerusalem and an MBA from the American University in Washington, D.C. Deafened in her thirties, she relearned how to navigate social, professional, and family relationships, and has chronicled this process through articles in newsletters, magazines, and in an anthology. She has worked in peer support services, community relations, and as an advocate for the deaf and hard of hearing.

Upon completing a full-length work of fiction which she is currently working to get published, Linda has filled her time with writing poetry; childhood memories of her parents joyfully reciting poems reignited her love of the art form. Her poems are published with Prompt for the Press; Viewless Wings Publisher; Wingless Dreamer's *Field of Black Roses, Vanish in Poetry, Ink the Universe, Summer Fireflies, Crystalline Whispers* and *Unveil the Memories* anthologies; Las Positas College's 2022 and 2023 *Havik* anthologies; *Bubble Literary Magazine;* and California Writers Club's Redwood Branch's *Phases* anthology. Her short fiction was published by the California Writers Club/ Tri-Valley Writers anthology, *Voices of the Valley—Through the Window.* She is the co-author of a children's picture book about isolation and feelings of otherness—*Who Wants to be Friends With a Dragon?*

Linda's aging horse and goats provided muses for many of her poems. She is a long-distance runner and writes poems of her experiences passing through local parks. Writing also has helped her overcome trauma; caught in the middle of a terror attack in 2016 in Nice, Paris, writing enabled her to process that event's impact on her life.

Linda resides in the city of Pleasanton and serves on the boards of both the California Communications Access Foundation and the California Writers Club/Tri-Valley Writers Branch. She may be reached through her Twitter handle @LindaDrattell. To learn more about Linda, visit *www. LindaDrattell.com.*

Printed in the USA
CPSIA information can be obtained
at www.ICGtesting.com
JSHW020315090224
56974JS00003B/143

9 798888 383254